Monkey is hiding

GW01464465

By Annette Smith

Here comes Monkey.

Look at Monkey.

Little Teddy is looking for Monkey.

Little Teddy

can not see Monkey.

Rabbit is looking
for Monkey.

Rabbit can not see Monkey.

Here comes Monkey.

Look at Monkey

and Little Teddy and Rabbit.